Collateral Damage
in the Marcellus Shale

by Walter M. Brasch

photos by Wendy Lynne Lee

Greeley & Stone, Publishers, LLC
Carmichael, California 95608

LCCN 2013943953
ISBN 978-0-942991-21-5

Design: MaryJayne Reibsome

PRINTED IN THE UNITED STATES OF AMERICA

Greeley & Stone, Publishers, LLC
4731 Whitney Ave., suite 20
Carmichael, Calif. 95608
www.greeleyandstone.com

Acknowledgements

Rosemary R. Brasch, as always, read the manuscript and provided excellent assistance and advice.

The staff of Greeley & Stone, Publishers, may be the best author-friendly professional staff in publishing. The assistance of Morris Stone (editor/publisher), MaryJayne Reibsome (art and production), Diana Saavedra (marketing and promotion), and Corey Ellen (business operations) is appreciated more than they can ever know.

More than 50 persons—college students, workers of all kinds, and the retired—for two weeks became a part of the Riverdale Mobile Home Village, protesting for citizen rights and against the infringement of the fracking industry upon the people, their health, and their environment.

But most of all, this book would never have been possible without the help and cooperation of the 32 families of Riverdale who were jerked into a reality they never expected. Their reality and their problem became our problem, and helped lead all of us to a better understanding about a part of our society.

PHOTO: Diane Siegmund

A rig in Bradford County, Pa.

4

PHOTO: Gary F. Clark

A platform on a rig near Warrensville, Pa.

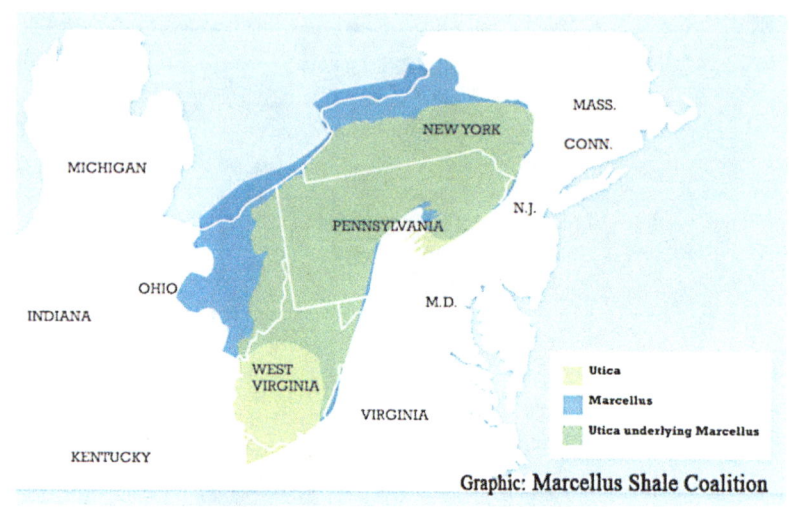

Graphic: Marcellus Shale Coalition

Utica
Marcellus
Utica underlying Marcellus

Commonwealth of Pennsylvania
Department of Environmental Protection
Bureau of Oil and Gas Management

Marcellus Shale Formation

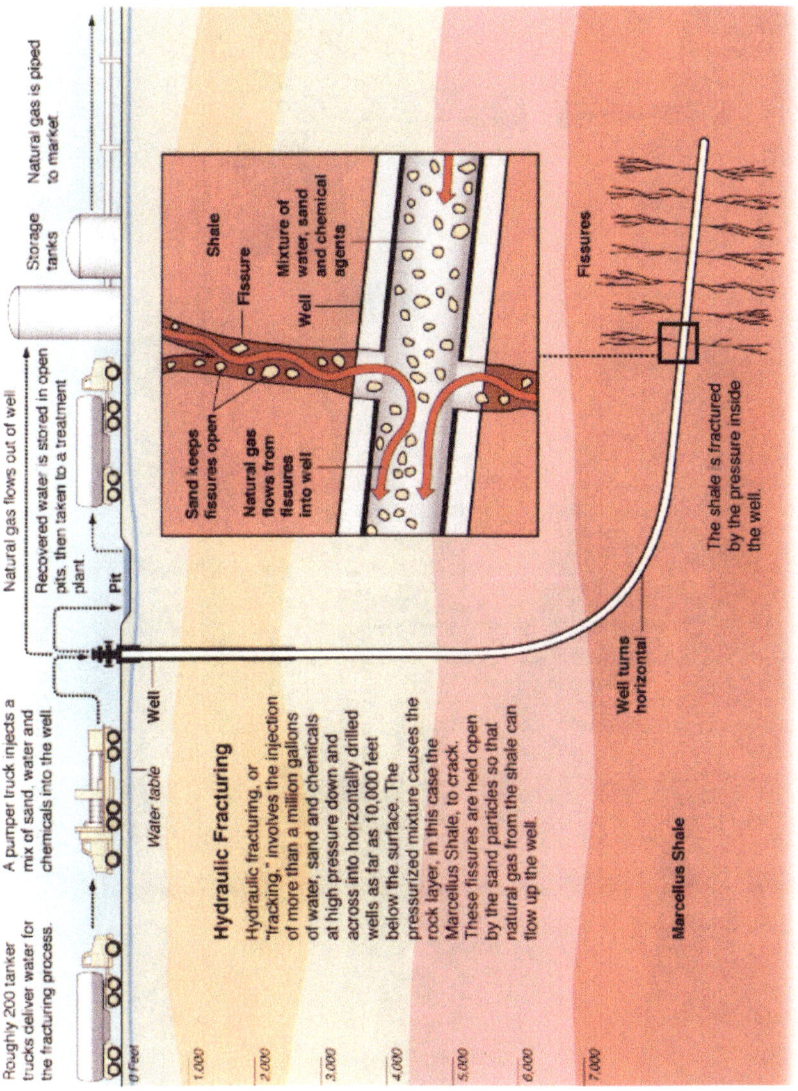

Roughly 200 tanker trucks deliver water for the fracturing process.

A pumper truck injects a mix of sand, water and chemicals into the well.

Natural gas flows out of well

Recovered water is stored in open pits, then taken to a treatment plant.

Storage tanks

Natural gas is piped to market.

Pit

Water table

Well

Hydraulic Fracturing

Hydraulic fracturing, or "fracking," involves the injection of more than a million gallons of water, sand and chemicals at high pressure down and across into horizontally drilled wells as far as 10,000 feet below the surface. The pressurized mixture causes the rock layer, in this case the Marcellus Shale, to crack. These fissures are held open by the sand particles so that natural gas from the shale can flow up the well.

Well turns horizontal

Marcellus Shale

The shale is fractured by the pressure inside the well.

Fissures

Shale

Fissure

Well

Mixture of water, sand and chemical agents

Sand keeps fissures open

Natural gas flows from fissures into well

0 Feet
1,000
2,000
3,000
4,000
5,000
6,000
7,000

Graphic by Al Granberg

7

A rig and pad dominate a farm and agricultural land near Troy, Pa.

Introduction

For National Drinking Water Week (May 5–11, 2013), the Pennsylvania Department of Environmental Protection (DEP) issued a press release to ask Pennsylvanians not only "to make every drop count," but also to "to learn how to better protect and conserve their water."

The release gave a few brief suggestions of how "to keep pollution out of water sources," and how "to conserve Pennsylvania's water sources." The release even gave a huge puff to Gov. Tom Corbett whom it said "is committed to water protecttion efforts that are vital to ensuring the health of the public and Pennsylvania's economy."[1]

Here are a few things the release did not state.

Corbett, two months after he took office in January 2011, declared he wanted to "make Pennsylvania the Texas of the natural gas boom."[2] To do that meant he and the Republican-controlled legislature had to create, with the help of the conservative American Legislative Exchange Council (ALEC), what became Act 13,[3] which Corbett signed on Valentine's Day 2012. It was a sweetheart gift to the natural gas exploration industry, the same one that had donated more than $1.8 million to Corbett's political campaigns.[4]

And so the state officially recognized and encouraged the development of high-volume hydraulic horizontal fracturing. Fracking, as the process is better known, is the controversial method of drilling into a rock formation as deep as 12,000 feet below the earth's surface. After drilling down vertically, the company sends fracking tubing, which has small explosive charges in it, to create a perforated lateral borehole, about 90 degrees from the vertical hole, which fractures the shale and rock for up to about 6,000 feet to open channels and force out natural gas and fossil fuels. Proppants, as much as 10,000 tons of silica sand,[5] keep the fractures open to allow the gas to flow from the shale into the well bore. Chemical additives, most of them toxic and labeled as carcinogens, prevent pipe corrosion and help force the sand and water into the site. Each well requires between three and nine million gallons of fresh water for the first frack, although Encana Oil & Gas USA used more than 21 million gallons of water to frack one well in Michigan in 2013.[6] The water is provided by companies that draw up to three million gallons a day from rivers and lakes, by individuals who sell water from their ponds, and by municipalities and water districts. There are more than 500,000 active wells in the United States,[7] each of which can be fracked several times.

Several shales in the United States contain natural gas—Barnett and Barnett–Woodford shales in Texas; Bakken shale in North Dakota and Saskatchewan; Fayetteville shale in Arkansas; Haynesville and Eagle Ford shales in the Louisiana area; Mancos and Lewis shales in the San Juan Basin in New Mexico, Colorado, and parts of Utah; the Monterey Shale in California's San Joaquin Basin, which yields primarily oil and some gas through conventional drilling methods; the South Georgia Basin in South Carolina, Georgia, and northern Florida; the New Albany Shale in the Illinois basin; the Woodford Shale in Oklahoma; the Chattanooga Shale in Tennessee; several smaller shales along the East Coast from Delaware into South Carolina; the South Newark Basin, which extends through parts of New Jersey and southern Pennsylvania; the Utica Shale, a deeper shale which ranges from parts of Ontario and Quebec in Canada, through parts of New York, Pennsylvania, Ohio, and West Virginia; and the Marcellus Shale, about 95,000 square miles.[8] Overall, at the end of 2012, there was about 482 trillion cubic feet of technically recoverable gas in all the shales, according to the Energy Information Administration. About 30 percent of that (141 tcf), according to the EIA, is believed to be recoverable in the Marcellus Shale.[9] During 2012, the Marcellus Shale yielded about seven billion cubic feet of gas a day, about one-fourth of the nation's gas production.[10] The top three plays—Haynesville, Barnett, and Marcellus—account for about two-thirds of all gas production.[11]

The Marcellus Shale—which extends beneath the Allegheny Plateau, through southern New York, much of Pennsylvania, east Ohio, West Virginia, and parts of Maryland and Virginia—

lies on top of the Devonian and Utica shales. The Marcellus Shale was created during the Middle Devonian epoch, about 400 million years ago. Also known as the Marcellus Formation, the Marcellus Shale was named by geologist James Hall in 1839 for Marcellus, N.Y., a small village near Syracuse, where an outcrop of the shale was first discovered.[12] (An outcrop is a geological formation that is usually covered by soil and vegetation but is exposed by erosion.) The recoverable gas in the Marcellus Shale is between 40[13] and 900[14] feet thick; gas in the shale is trapped between impervious layers of limestone.

Contrary to some industry claims that natural gas could provide energy for more than a century, the reality is that not only is fossil fuel a finite source of energy, but that it may provide only enough for a couple of decades. The high-end estimates do not take into consideration that at present only 10–15 percent of all natural gas in the Marcellus Shale is viable; the costs to go after the rest of the available gas may not be financially justified if gas prices to consumers have to increase significantly, says Karen Feridun of Berks Gas Truth.

Advocates of fracking argue natural gas is "greener" than coal and oil energy, with significantly fewer carbon, nitrogen, and sulfur emissions. But, there are other realities. First, escaped methane from natural gas released into the air and water increase problems with public health and the environment; second, production and distribution errors and problems mining natural gas make it the equivalent of coal and oil.

About 78 percent of unprocessed natural gas is methane (CH_4),[15] the simplest hydrocarbon and one of the major contributors to ozone layer depletion. "[W]hen released directly into the atmosphere [methane] is a potent greenhouse gas—more than 20 times more potent than carbon dioxide," according to Lisa Jackson, a chemical engineer and Environmental Protection Agency administrator, 2009–2013.[16] There are two kinds of methane—biogenic and thermogenic. Biogenic gas, lying closer to the surface, is produced by methanogenic organisms as a metabolic byproduct. Thermogenic gas, deeper in the earth, is composed of organic decomposition that is affected by heat and pressure Although methane isn't toxic, it is flammable and explosive, and can migrate into aquifers and wells.[17]

The shale gas industry claims fracking has been proven safe

for more than six decades. What it doesn't publicly say is that it is *vertical* fracking, which uses significantly less water and toxic fluids than *horizontal* fracking, that has a better safety record. Horizontal fracking, a brilliant engineering triumph that only became commercially viable about 2006, has numerus problems. Further, because the term "fracking" is commonly used to refer to the entire process, rather than one part, the natural gas industry has tried to convince the public that fracking isn't as dangerous as people believe, conveniently leaving out problems in other parts of the process that include not just drilling, but extracting, refining, storing, and trans-porting.

About half of all water and various elements, dissolved solids, and chemicals—known variously as wastewater, flowback, blow-back, or brine, saltier than seawater—is brought to the surface and must be disposed. In most drilling operations, this flowback is captured in storage tanks or ponds, where it is pumped into tanker trucks for disposal at sewage facilities, or injected into deep wells. In some cases, it just lies in unprotected open ponds. The rest of the mixture stays within the ground, some-times affecting water supplies; however, that part, contamiated with fracking chemicals, will eventually come to the surface.

Now, let's pretend each well pad and the associated infra-structure (roads, pipelines, *etc.*), which carve out eight acres, don't contribute to fragmentation that affects wildlife and the ecological balance of nature.

Let's also pretend that the water brought up from fracking doesn't contain chemicals, compounds, and radioactive waste that were disturbed by the process. And, let's pretend that the billions of gallons of this toxic mixture brought up isn't put into open storage pits, where it could evaporate into the air or leak from plastic liners of the pits and into the ground. And, let's pretend there are no problems with the current method to get rid of that toxic waste that is injected back into the ground, and that doing so won't cause more pollution and, possibly, a series of small earthquakes.

And, let's pretend there isn't a 7 percent failure of the cement casings that, at least in theory, protect the billions of gallons of water, toxic fluids, and sand from leaking into the earth or that within two decades all casings will deteriorate. And, let's pretend there can never be any migration of all that toxic fluid into aquifers and somehow into the wells of about two million Pennsylvanians.

Let's stretch our level of credulity and pretend there is no air, water, or ground pollution, and that there are no health and environmental effects from fracking. And, let's really stretch our level of naiveté and pretend that like water used by farmers that goes into the ground or air and can be recycled, or the massive amounts of water that is used by nuclear plants and which can be recycled, or that water used by individuals that is flushed into a sewer plant, processed, and then returned to the earth, that the wastewater of fracking is also reusable.

Disregard the evidence, and accept what we are told by the industry and politicians, who swear upon stacks of $100 bills, that fracking is safe and controlled. There is still the question of water, the most critical part of fracking.

Energy companies drilling Pennsylvania use the second greatest amount of water, behind Texas and followed by Colorado and Arkansas.[18]

Beginning about 2008, the water in the nation's aquifers has been decreasing significantly. This depletion, according to Leonard Konikow, a research hydrologist at the U.S. Geological Survey. is about three times the rate as between 1900 through 2008.[19]

Significant reductions in water availability are now common for the 1,450 mile long Colorado River, which provides water to about 40 million people in California and the southwest, including the agriculture-rich Imperial Desert of southeastern California. Lake Mead, a part of the Colorado system, provides water to Las Vegas and the Nevada desert communities; its water level is close to the point where the U.S. Department of the Interior will declare a water shortage and impose strict water-use regulation.[20]

The depletion of the rivers, lakes, and aquifers is because of population growth, higher usage, climate change, and a severe drought that has spread throughout the Midwest and southwest for the past three years.

Water is so critical to the fracking process that during the drought in the Midwest and Southwest oil and gas companies are buying water from farmers and municipalities and trucking it to the drilling fields from as far away as Pennsylvania.[21] Agriculture fields and, sometimes, livestock suffer because the industry needs water, and is paying premium prices, as much as $1,000–$2,000 for about 326,000 gallons (an acre foot);[22] the normal price is about $30–$100 for the same amount. In most cases, the natural gas industry is able to outbid farmers for water supplies.

The Coalition for Environmentally Responsible Economies (CERES), basing its analysis upon more than 25,000 wells, reports almost 47 percent of wells that use fracking were developed in areas with high or extremely high water stress levels; 92 percent of all gas wells in Colorado are in extremely high-stressed regions; In Texas, 51 percent are in high or extremely high stress water regions.[23]

In 2005, there were only eight unconventional wells in Pennsylvania. By the end of 2012, there were 6,258 wells.[24] That would mean at least 44 billion gallons of water, most of it taken from the state's rivers, was used to frack the environment. That doesn't include all the water that is spilled and unusable. So, while the Commonwealth of Pennsylvania wants individuals to conserve every drop of water, it is also encouraging out-of-state megacorporations to grab as much as they can in order to continue to frack the state.

The last sentence of the DEP press release may be the most important. "This year," say the DEP's PR people, "marks the 39th anniversary of the Safe Water Drinking Act, the main federal law that ensures the quality of drinking water in the United States."

But the Safe Water Drinking Act doesn't apply to the natural gas industry. In 2005—by a 249–183 vote in the House and an 85–12 vote in the Senate—Congress exempted the oil and natural gas industry from the Safe Water Drinking Act. That exemption applied to the "construction of new well pads and the accompanying new roads and pipelines."

The fracking industry, also by Congressional action, mostly during the George W. Bush Administration, is also exempt from all or parts of the National Environmental Policy Act, Clean Air Act, Clean Water Act, and the Resource Conservation and Recovery Act.

Another federal law that protects Americans is the Comprehensive Environmental Response, Compensation, and Liability Act (CERCLA), which created the "superfund" that holds companies financially liable for polluting the environment. However, Congress specifically exempted oil and natural gas industries from CERCLA.

Dick Cheney, whose promotion of Big Business and opposition to environmental policies is well-documented, had pushed for the exemptions while he was vice-president. His hand-picked "energy task force," composed primarily of industry representatives, had concluded that fracking was safe. Cheney had been CEO of Halliburton, one of the world's largest energy companies, headquartered in both Houston, Texas, and Dubai; the exemptions from clean water and air protections is known as the Halliburton Loophole.

The DEP and the Corbett Administration can issue all the press releases they want. But they can't deny the reality that while they want individuals to save every drop of water, the state officially encourages the use and waste of water in its mindless race to excavate all the gas it can get—in the false assumption it will create jobs, improve the economy, lower gas prices, and make the U.S. energy independent—but at the cost of the health of the people, tainting their food source, and destruction of their environment.

It's this need for water why 32 families were evicted from their homes in Jersey Shore, Pa.

This is their story.

PHOTO: Robert Donnan
A convoy of trucks blocks traffic near Dryden, Pa.
It's a common scene throughout the Marcellus Shale.

PART 1
MARCH 2012

There's nothing to suggest that in his 51 years Kevin June should be a leader.

Not from his high school where he dropped out after his freshman year.

Not from his job, where he worked as an auto body technician more than 35 years.

Both of his marriages ended in divorce, but did produce two children, a 31-year-old son and a 28-year-old daughter.

June readily admits that for most of his life, beginning about 14 when he began drinking heavily, he was a drunk. Always beer. Almost always to excess. But, he will quickly tell you how many weeks he has been sober. It's now been 56 weeks, he proudly says.

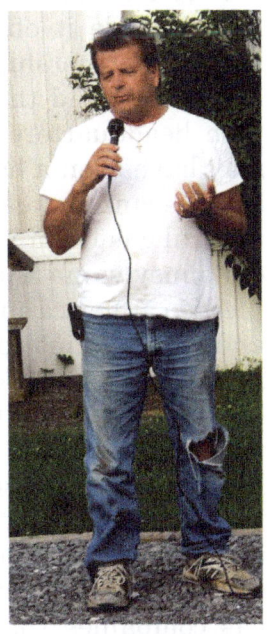

In October 2008 he was in an auto accident when he swerved to miss a deer and hit an oak tree head on. That's when he learned MRIs revealed he had been suffering from degenerative arthritis. Between the accident and the arthritis, he was off work for three months. Then, in May 2009, he was laid off when the company moved.

Kevin June

Unable to work, surviving on disability income that brings him $1,300 a month, just $392.50 above the poverty line, he lives in the Riverdale Mobile Home Village, along the Susquehanna River near Jersey Shore, about 20 miles west of Williamsport, in north-central Pennsylvania. The village has a large green area where families can picnic, relax, and play games, sharing the space with geese and all kinds of animals and natural vegetation.

For most of the six years June lived in the village, he kept to himself—chatting with neighbors now and then, but nothing that would ever suggest he'd be a leader. The last time he led anything was almost two decades earlier when he was president of a 4-wheel club.

On Feb. 18, 2012, the residents found out after reading a story in the Williamsport *Sun-Gazette* their village had been sold and would be demolished. The owner/landlord, Richard A. (Skip) Leonard, later came to each of the 32 families, told them he sold the 12.5 acre park, and they would have two months to leave. It was abrupt. Business-like. "For Sale" signs had been posted at the property almost four years. Kevin June says the residents knew Leonard was planning to sell, "but we thought it would be to someone who would allow us to stay."

Four days after the residents were ordered to move, certified letters made it official. Leonard had sold the park to Aqua–PVR, a partnership of Aqua America, headquartered in Bryn Mawr, Pa., and the smaller Penn Virginia Resource Partners, with headquarters in Radnor, Pa. Sale price was $550,000. It may have been a bargain—land and industrial parks that have been vacant for years are going for premium sales prices as the natural gas boom in the Marcellus Shale consumes a large part of Pennsylvania and four surrounding states.

Aqua America provides water to about 2.8 million residents and corporations in nine states, including about 1.4 million in Pennsylvania.[25] It had received permission from the Susquehanna River Basin Commission (SRBC) to withdraw up to three million gallons of water a day for 15 years from the West Branch of the Susquehanna; the families of the mobile home village would just be in the way. The company intends to initially spend about $20 million to build a pump station and create an 18-mile pipe system to provide fresh water to natural gas companies that use hydraulic fracturing.[26] The pumping station will be between two others, both owned by Anadarko Petroleum, both taking water from the Susquehanna. About a mile downstream, one pumping station is authorized to take up to 1.5 million gallons of water a day; upstream, another is authorized to take up to 720,000 gallons a day.

While the Delaware River Basin Commission, and the states

of New York and New Jersey have imposed moratoriums upon the use of fracking until full health and environmental impacts can be assessed, Pennsylvania and the SRBC have been handing out permits by the gross.

Leonard says he tried to sell the land to someone who would keep the village, and allow the residents to remain. "I had a legitimate buyer who owned a large mobile home park," he says, but backed out of the deal when he saw the requirements imposed by the Lycoming County Zoning Hearing Board. The Board, says Leonard, required new tenants of the park, which was in a flood zone, to raise their trailers 12 feet. Doing so would make the trailers inaccessible to anyone with a physical handicap and cost at least $5,000 per trailer to elevate. He says he had letters from the Federal Emergency Management Agency that exempted the trailer park from that requirement, "and the Board said it would check with FEMA to verify it." However, says Leonard, the Board didn't check with FEMA but with the state's Insurance Commission, which reaffirmed the Board's contention that trailers had to be elevated 12 feet. "I tried fighting this for over a year," says Leonard, but the Board didn't care. And then Aqua America came along, "and I took their offer."

David Hine, Lycoming County zoning administrator, confirms FEMA regulations that require "any new trailer that is put onto the property be elevated 12 feet," one and one-half feet above the 100-year flood elevation, "and that applies to anyone in the flood plain." He says Leonard is right about existing trailers being "grandfathered," but new trailers would have had to meet the elevation requirements. Raising trailers 12 feet, says Hine, "can be done; it just takes some engineering." Hine says the Zoning Board isn't concerned about problems of handicap accessibility because "it doesn't apply to one or two family dwellings."

Daniel Fitzpatrick, local government policy specialist with the Pennsylvania Department of Community and Economic Development, reinforces Hine's statements:

> "Minimum regulations under the National Flood Insurance Program that are contained in a municipality's flood plain management ordinance require that new residential construction in an identified Special Flood Hazard Area be elevated so that the lowest floor is at or above the elevation of

the 1% Annual Chance Flood. Placement of manufactured homes qualifies as new construction under the regulations of the program. Failure of a municipality to enforce the regulations in their ordinance could ultimately result in suspension from the program. Placement of manufactured homes in the flood plain is one of the most dangerous types of development and therefore should receive special attention for compliance."

Some believe there may have been a backroom deal between the zoning commissioners and the natural gas industry, which was becoming ubiquitous in the county. "That's nonsense," says Hine.

Most residents had only a vague knowledge of fracking and what it is doing to the earth. Deb Eck says she "knew nothing" about fracking, "so I 'Googled' it, and up came thousands of hits." She says she "learned real fast" what it was, and what it was doing to the people and the land. Kevin June says the residents of Riverdale "have a lot more knowledge now."

PART 2
APRIL 2012

Aqua had originally ordered the residents to leave by May 1, but then extended it to the end of the month. It dangled a $2,500 relocation allowance in its eviction. However, the cost to move a trailer to another park is $6,000–$11,000, plus extra for skirting, sheds, and any handicap-accessible external ramps. About a third of the trailers can't be moved.

"These are older trailers," says Kevin June. His trailer is a 12-by-70, built in 1974, with a tin roof and tin siding ("tin-on-tin"). Most of the trailers aren't sturdy enough to survive a move. But even if all could be moved, there are few places that would take the other families. The parks want the newer trailers, but most parks are full. So, the residents are desperately reading the classified ads for rentals.

Because the natural gas companies are bringing thousands of employees to frack the land, there is a shortage of apartments; most landlords have increased rents to take advantage of the well-paid roustabouts, drivers, technicians, engineers and other professionals who moved into the area, and spend their money on local businesses eager to improve their own profits. During the past two years, rents have doubled and tripled. "None of us can pay a thousand or more a month," says June. The current mobile home owners paid $200 a month for their lot.

The gas drilling boom that hit Pennsylvania has resulted in an increase in the number of homeless, many of whom were evicted at the end of their leases by landlords who wanted to make apartments available for gas field workers willing to pay higher rents. Many of the homeless, unable to find housing or qualify for jobs in the gas fields, have placed an additional burden upon social service agencies; other homeless, even if employed, are invisible to the people and governments of their communities.

Not long after he was served his own eviction notice, June had a dream. "It was Jesus coming to me, telling me I had to do something," he says. And so, Kevin June became their unofficial leader. If something goes wrong, the residents have to fix it or call June. If he can't fix a problem, he finds someone who can. In this trailer park, as in most communities, there is a lot of talent—"we help each other," says June. "I've had the Holy Spirit running through my veins a long time, but it's running real deep right now," he says.

June is constantly on the move, going from trailer to trailer to try to keep the residents informed, to help families who were abruptly evicted. Whatever their needs, Kevin June tries to provide it. He's constantly on the phone, running up phone bills he knows he can't afford but does so anyhow because the lives of his neighbors matter.

There's Betty and William Whyne. Betty, 82, began working as a waitress at the age of 13 and now, in retirement, makes artificial Christmas trees. She has a cancerous tumor in the same place where a breast was removed in 1991. William, 72, who was an electrician, carpenter, and plumber before he retired after a heart attack, goes to a dialysis center three times a week, four hours each time. They brought their 12-wide 1965 Fleetwood trailer to the village shortly after the 1972 flood. Like the other residents, they can't afford to move; they can't find adequate housing. "We've looked at everything in about a 30 mile radius," they say. They earn $1,478 a month from retirement, only $252.17 above the federal poverty line.[27]

One son is in New Jersey, one is in Texas; the Whynes don't want to leave the area; they shouldn't have to.

There's April and Eric Daniels. She's a stay-at-home mom for their two children; he's a truck driver for Stallion Oilfield Services, delivering water to natural gas companies in Pennsylvania and wastewater into Ohio. Their 14-by-76 foot trailer, which they bought in 2009, is now valued at $13,200; she and her husband were in the process of remodeling it, had already paid $8,000 for improvements in two years, and were about to start building a second bathroom. April Daniels had grown up living in a series of foster houses, "so I know what it's like to move around, but this was my first home, and it's harder for me to leave." Their trailer provides a good home, but can't be moved. "We're pretty much on the verge of just tearing down the trailer and living in a camper," she says. They don't know what will happen. They do know that because of what they see as Aqua's insensitivity, they will lose a lot of money no matter what they do.

Doris Fravel, 82, a widow on a fixed income of $1,326 a month, lived in the village 38 years. She's proud of her 1974 12-wide trailer with the tin roof. "I painted it every year," she says. Eight months earlier, she paid $3,580 for a new air conditioner; she recently paid $3,000 for new insulated skirting. The trailer has new carpeting. Unlike most of the residents, she found housing—a $450 a month efficiency, which she says she likes. But it's far smaller than her current home. So she's sold or

PHOTO: Alex Lotorto

Betty and William Whyne

given away most of what she owns. She may have a buyer for the trailer, but will take Aqua America's offer of $2,500 for it, considerably less than it's worth. "I can't do anything else," she says. "I just can't move my furnishings into the new apartment," she says. Like the other residents, she has family who are helping, but there's only so much help any family can provide. "I never knew I would ever have to leave," she says, but she does want to "see one of those gas men come to my door—and I'd like to punch him in the shoulder."

Not only are there few lots available and apartments are too expensive, but most residents don't qualify for a mortgage; and there are waiting lists for senior citizen and low-income housing. The stories are the same.

No one from Aqua has been in touch with any resident. "If they would just have come out here and talked with us like they were supposed to, there might not have been problems," says April Daniels. But, the company did hire a local real estate agency. The agency claims it has made extraordinary efforts to help the residents find other housing. The residents disagree. April Daniels says "some of the Realtors have gotten real nasty with the people in the park—they just don't understand that we are all in a hardship, so we get mad and frustrated and take it out on them." But there really isn't much anyone can do. The natural gas boom has made affordable housing as obsolete as the anthracite coal that once drove the region's energy economy.

The residents, with limited incomes, have lived good lives; they are good people. They paid their rents and fees on time; they kept up the appearances of their trailers and the land around it. They worked their jobs; they survived. Until they were evicted.

And now it's up to the residents to try to survive. They have become closer; they listen to each other; they hug each other; and the tough men aren't afraid to let others see them cry. "The pain in this park is almost too much at times," says Kevin June.

Most of the families see their eviction as a politically-based corporate takeover. June says he went to see State Rep. Garth Everett (R-Muncy) "to ask what he could do to help, but his secretary just coldly told me there was nothing that could be done because whoever owns a property can do with it what he wants to do." He never saw the state representative.

During the week Aqua–PVR issued eviction notices, its parent company issued a news release, boasting that its revenue for 2011 was $712 million, a 4.2 percent increase from the year before; its net income was $143.1 million, up 15.4 percent from the previous year.[28] Two months later, Penn Virginia Resource Partners, which had teamed with Aqua America to buy and level Riverdale and to develop a pumping station, bought Chief Gathering, an energy pipeline company, for $1.06 billion.[29] But, for some reason, the company just couldn't find enough money to give the residents a fair moving settlement. "They just expect us to throw our homes into the street and live in tents," says June.

PART 3
MAY 2012

The forced eviction had united the residents, but by the middle of May, most reluctantly took the $2,500 relocation allowance and left the village.

"I was scared of what they would do, because they had the lawyers and the money," says Fred Kinley, a 79-year old Air Force veteran and retired sheet metal worker, who was one of the last to leave before the May 31 deadline. Kinley had lived in his 1970 12-by-70 foot trailer for 27 years, which he couldn't move for the $2,500 he was offered. "I had no place to move," he says, "and was running out of time." And so he abandoned his trailer, and moved into a trailer park about eight miles away, where he is paying $450 a month to rent a trailer that "isn't nearly as nice as the one I had owned." The one he owned would remain at Riverdale.

Other residents stripped their trailers of pipes, fixtures, and porches, anything that could be taken and used in a new home, anything that could be sold, anything that other residents might be able to use.

Seven families remained to fight what they saw as an injustice.

Kevin June, becoming adept at how to work with the media, was constantly calling radio and TV stations and newspapers, and working the social media, especially Twitter and Facebook. Alex Lotorto, a grounds technician and volunteer from nearby

Lewisburg, Pa., set up a website, SaveRiverdale,[30] with information and photos. The pleas and stories drew assistance from anti-fracking groups Clean Water Action, Earth First, Gas Drilling Awareness Coalition, and Responsible Drilling Alliance. Soon a nation was able to see micro-documentaries on YouTube, posted by several amateur videojournalists, including Dean Marshall and Cris McConkey, and organizations, among them the Media Mobilizing Project. Photojournalist Lynn Johnson, who is working on a story about the women of the Marcellus Shale for *National Geographic*, was in Riverdale to photograph that community's life.

Several readers of the Williamsport *Sun-Gazette* wrote letters to the editor or posted their comments to the online site of the newspaper to show their support for the residents of Riverdale.

"I question why the SRBC [Susquehanna River Basin Commission] shows preferential treatment to fretful, whining cries of the gas companies while initiating stress, hardships and inexcusable moving expenses onto families who cannot afford the financial burden to relocate," wrote Weldon C. Cohick Jr., whose ancestors lived in the township for two centuries.[31]

One reader, who identified herself only as Miss Jane, in an online comment noted that her mother went through similar proceedings in Florida. The residents, she said, "were only given 6 weeks notice. [It] got real bad towards the end [when] the company who bought the land did not wait til all the tenants left to start decimating empty trailers. [W]e woke up everyday to terrible destructive noises of units being ripped apart."[32]

Billtown 101 said he would like to know:

"if the commissioners who approved these plans gave as much consideration to the lives and well-being of those 'Families', as they so quickly accepted a 'Waiver' to overlook the Land Development Ordinance regarding the increased slope of the access road—which will potentially cause storm-water runoff issues? I highly doubt the truck traffic issue played a major role in the selling of your souls. God Bless these families, and I pray that each of you some how will find a greater understanding and Compassion from your local neighbors than you have by the blindness of your local government leaders and the greed of the cold-heart."

However, in the center of the Marcellus Shale boom, most of the neighbors and readers of the *Sun-Gazette* condemned the residents who had complained about their sudden eviction, and who refuse to leave until they receive what they believe should be fair compensation.

The harpies who wrote several hundred posts that appeared online in the *Sun-Gazette* were relentless in their condemnation of the residents. Hiding behind anonymous screen names, the writers, who sound like drunks in a bar fight or callers to an afternoon talk show, could be among thousands of employees and managers, many from Texas and Oklahoma, who have temporarily moved into the area. They could be the landlords who raised their rents three and four times to take advantage of the incoming gas field workers. They could be those who have leased part of their land to the oil companies. They could also be the business owners who have profited because of selling products to the workers. But most of them condemned the residents.

Garder54 called Kevin June "a real scum."

LadyDawg4 called him a "sleazeball."

Proud2bMom called him a "liar and a thief."

Linhk48, who posted several dozen times, believes "the new owner's only obligation is to give you notice to vacate. He is under absolutely no obligation to subsidize your move, allow you to live rent free until you move, or hire professionals to help you with relocation. Anything he does is a generosity and SHOULD be appreciated!" Linhk48 thought Aqua–PVR should take the residents to court "for leaving the property with trailer shells and trash all over and ask for clean-up costs—and punitive damages after they were so generous." Linhk48, like many, called them "rabble-Rousers/troublemakers/trespassers."

Czkb217 thought the police or National Guard could move in, and advised the residents, "SO just pack your stuff and MOVE, you are now breaking the law." It's doubtful any of the commentators know Pennsylvania state law that establishes legal processes that must be met to evict persons from their homes.

CitizenQ, who opposes helping the residents and who posted several times, without evidence claimed "some of the residents have been seen stealing from others."

Several repeatedly questioned where the donations to River-dale went. Some specifically accused Kevin June of theft and fraud, apparently not having the time or intelligence to learn about the controls and regulations to release money from a bank-held account that is a registered 501(c) charity. "The residents know exactly where the money went and why," says June.

When those writing to the *Sun-Gazette* later learned some of the money was used to buy phone cards, a camera, a weed whacker, and a used $200 riding lawnmower, they increased their assault. Had they taken the time to think or ask questions—something those who type and pound "SEND" often don't do—they would have learned that June used the phone cards to cover many of his expenses from numerous cell phone calls to and from attorneys, the media, and others who had an interest in the problems of the residents. They would have learned that June bought the camera because the lawyers required him to document the appearance of the village and the residents' activities. They would have learned that June bought lawn and gardening equipment because both the previous and new owners had no intention of mowing the lawns or killing the weeds. Cutting grass and eliminating weeds also served to help protect their health; living near the river, with the warm seasons approaching, residents knew there would be increased black fly and mosquito infestations.

Woolrich haughtily wanted to know, "Why on earth would you not have saved money for when you eventually had to move your MOBILE home???" Perhaps, Woolrich, it's because when you have poverty-level income, it's hard to save anything.

No2spanish believed, "[T]his is why people in mobile homes should save their money—instead of spending it on booze or drugs."

Czkb217 thought the residents should have gotten together and bought the park. Since most of the families live slightly above the poverty line, they probably don't have an extra $550,000 plus lawyer fees and closing costs laying around. Nevertheless, Czkb217 believes the residents should "Just man up and put your big boy panties on and MOVE." He objects that his taxes are supporting some of the residents who are using Legal Aid, which receives state and federal funds to assist the impoverished. John Person with the Williamsport office of North Penn Legal Services and Kevin Quisenberry of the Community Justice Project in Pittsburgh assisted the low-income residents of the village; Jonathan Butterfield of the Williamsport law firm of Murphy, Butterfield and Holland assisted *pro bono* for those residents who didn't qualify for legal services.

Justin1 wanted the residents to "Get out of the way of progress already."

Ironically, many of those who support the fracking industry will soon find out that the new pump station will lead to a loss of well-paying jobs. Aqua–PVR proudly says the new station would be more environmentally friendly since it would remove about 1,000 water hauling trucks per day from the roads.[33]

Many of those who attack the residents and defend corporations probably believe they are good Christians; they attend church regularly and, in one of the more conservative and highly Christian parts of the state, praise God publically.

However, the Rev. Leah Schade, who held an interfaith service at the village, doesn't see them as good Christians. "It is a craven, cowardly way to snipe at people," she says. Those criticizing the residents "are profiting from the way things are or they are so insulated from the pain and suffering the people are undergoing that they are unable to respond with compassion," says Rev. Schade, pastor of the United in Christ Lutheran Church in nearby Lewisburg. "As a Christian," she says, "I make a decision to do what Jesus calls us to do—to minister to those most vulnerable and resist the powers and the principalities that seek their own self perpetuation and their own profit." Rev. Schade, who is completing a Ph.D. in ecological theology, points out, "The church has a long history of offering a prophetic voice

The Rev. Leah Schade

28

to persons who are oppressed and made vulnerable by powerful systems, and who need advocates to speak for and alongside of them in the public arena. The teachings of Jesus would tell us that what is happening to these families isn't right. He would ask, 'Who controls the resources; who does not?' The residents and the surrounding ecosystem are the disempowered ones."

Shells of tin and fiber board, some with exposed asbestos, make the place 32 families once called home now looking like a battlefield.

"It's not the trailers that make up the community," says April Daniels, "it's the people who live in it."

PART 4
JUNE 2012

Aqua America didn't want a fight. It probably didn't even expect the myriad problems that had been dumped upon it.

The situation in Riverdale was becoming a public relations and operations disaster. It was David vs. Goliath, and no corporation wants to be seen as Goliath. But Aqua–PVR, under the Aqua America umbrella, wanted to begin construction of the pump station. Some of the Aqua executives had to have felt conflicted, maybe even confused—they had bought the land in good faith, and may not have had knowledge of the consequences; they couldn't understand why 32 families living in trailers would cause such a problem to a huge corporation that just wanted to build a pump station. "The guy ["Skip" Leonard] was supposed to have sold us a clean piece of property," Nick DeBenedictis, Aqua America's CEO, complained to the *Philadelphia Inquirer*.[34] Besides, Aqua America may have reasoned it wasn't even the one that was fracking the earth; it was merely pulling out water to send to those companies that did the fracking. What Aqua–PVR was doing was relatively clean. Even if it had consequences for the marine life and vegetation, a governmental body had approved its application to withdraw up to three million gallons a day. And now there was a problem that may have seemed greater than what the fracking companies were experiencing.

On Thursday, May 31, the final day residents were legally

Anti-fracking protestors meet at the banks of the West Branch of the Susquehanna River to discuss strategy to help the Riverdale residents.

allowed to remain in Riverdale, seven families remained in what was left of their micro-village. They were joined by 50 anti-fracking activists who showed up to begin a vigil. "We asked the residents about their concerns, explained what we wanted to do, and made sure what we wanted to do would help the residents and not cause them further harm," says Alex Lotorto, one of the protestors.

The next day, the day Aqua said it would begin construction, the protestors blockaded the two entrances to the park. The barriers included old washing machines, tires, cinder blocks, and fiber board, anything the protestors could take out of the trailers that were abandoned. What informally became known as the Occupation of Riverdale began Friday, June 1, 2012.

"It should never have gotten to a blockade," Lotorto says. But it did get to a blockade because of an intractable corporation that was determined to use the land it purchased to put up a pumping station, and it wanted no delay.

"We are here to fight against the exploitation and abandonment by a society of the economically vulnerable," said Dr. Wendy Lynne Lee, one of the protestors. "Our purpose was to protect the park's residents from unjust expulsion and to make people aware that this non-violent protest is against the egregious injustice of these evictions," said Dr. Lee.[35] Seven families remained in the park on the day Aqua had given its deadline.

"When we first heard about the protest," says Eric Daniels,

Anti-fracking protestors put up up a security tent.

31

"we [he and his wife, April] weren't very happy because anti-fracking protestors would throw rocks at my truck." However, Daniels quickly realized that these protestors weren't involved in destruction of property. "After sitting and talking with them [the Riverdale protestors] the first day, I realized they were working class people, just like we are. They were here to help us, brought food, shared their lives with us, and cleaned up after residents moved out."

While the residents and protestors were friendly, some of the residents didn't join the protest. Scott Bliler says he "just didn't want to do it." Toby Mainse and his fiancée Traci June, Kevin June's daughter, friends of "Skip" Leonard, refused to be a part of the protest, but had stayed in the village past the June 1 deadline.

Kevin June says the problems in the village for the residents were magnified not by Aqua but by how "Skip" Leonard nego-tiated the sales contract and the promises he had made to residents that even if he sold the land, none of the residents would have to leave. Kevin June's activism and the subsequent protest would cause further tension between Traci June and her father, with Traci not speaking to him at all.

Another reason some stayed away from the protest, although sharing their community with the protestors, was because they feared if they joined the protest, it would upset legal negotia-tions being held with Aqua America for increased compen-sation; Aqua itself had wanted a separation between residents and protestors.

Online comments by readers of the *Sun-Gazette* identified the protestors as "out-of-town activists" or, more specifically, "environmental activists." Bobbie2 called the scene a "liberal zoo . . . a veritable microcosm of the liberal social system." Joe123 called the protestors "unorganized morons," and decided the residents "are on display by 'Fame Seekers', like trick-monkeys in a circus." Proud2bMom, with no facts, something that never stymied any of the others who wrote into the online site, claimed "the residents left that are trying to get out are more or less being held prisoner in their own homes because of the few who feel they need to block the roads." Many, who had never been to the village, called the protestors unwashed hippies who were living off welfare and the government. However,

32

most protestors had jobs, and came to the village on their days off and in the evenings. Some were students from Oberlin College; some were retired.

Also attacking the protestors was Energy in Depth (EID), the public relations and propaganda operation formed by the energy industry. Tom Shepstone, campaign director for EID/ Northeast Marcellus Initiative, engaged in a continuing campaign to discredit the protestors. On the EID website, Shepstone claimed, "[T]he protestors are exploiting these people to make an ideological point about natural gas," and argued:

> "While the residents of the Riverdale park may think they have found supportive allies, in actuality they found a convenient partner that will be on to their next headline grabbing effort in quick fashion likely leaving Riverdale behind when this occurs."[36]

Deb Eck

By the middle of May, there was a subtle change in leadership. Kevin June had been the force to unite the residents and get the media and lawyers, but his communication skills were weak, and residents were becoming confused by what was and was not happening. Deb Eck became the liaison between protestors, residents, police, and on-site company workers. Eck focused upon helping the remaining Riverdale residents before she went to work as a manager of a retail store in Williamsport, worked long shifts, and then came home, usually about 9 or 10 p.m., and worked a few hours. "Some of my days I only got four hours of sleep," she says. June, still doing what he could for the residents, increased his work with the media and the lawyers.

On the sixth day of the protest, "Skip" Leonard, who still owned about 45 acres adjacent to the parcel he had sold, including some camping areas, rode into Riverdale on an orange Kubota tractor, with a front scoop-bucket attached, hit the barricade, an adjacent STOP sign, and almost hit George West, one of the protestors. "He hit it, backed up, hit it again and again," says Jackie Wilson, a retired secretary and one of the protestors. On a small mower deck attached to the tractor was a 4-foot x 8-foot plywood sign—"MAKE THE TRESPASSERS CLEAN UP THEIR MESS AND LEAVE!!!" That sign was later screwed onto a pole owned by Pennsylvania Power Light.

Wilson says she had asked a State Police sergeant for an incident report to report the damage, but he refused "and was nasty about it." She says "it was a rude awakening," because she had worked 19 years for the Springfield Twp. (Dauphin County) police department, "and never saw anyone treat a person like that."

The protestors and residents understood that Leonard, now retired after working 47 years in construction, was frustrated, upset that he was now seen as a villain who sold out a trailer park. The barriers blocked him from unrestricted access to another part of his property, and he wasn't afraid to make sure others knew he was blocked from a picnic area, even though the protestors removed parts of the barrier any time Leonard had previously showed up to allow him and others to have unobstructed access into and out of the park. "We were trying not to have any conflict with Mr. Leonard and others," says George Daniels, an organic farmer from Lewisburg, Pa., and one of the protestors.

"People were spreading his name around," says Alex Lotorto, "they were mad and upset themselves, they may have been harassing him in town, but the problem still goes back to the Susquehanna River Basin Commission that allowed Aqua America to take water."

But on that one day, the day he ran into a barrier, "Skip"

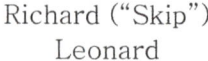
Richard ("Skip") Leonard

Leonard had had enough. He didn't want to have to go through protestors, who he thought were professional agitators, to reach his picnic area, no matter how easy or hard they had made it for him. Although he no longer owned the land that once was a small trailer park, he was disgusted by its appearance. For 28 years, he had done his best to maintain a park that was pleasant and physically attractive. But now, says Leonard, these protestors "were bringing every kind of garbage they could find and lined that barricade with it; it was disgusting." No police actions were taken against Leonard or the protestors.

Most of the residents of Riverdale had respected Leonard. "He was a stand-up guy who ran a safe and clean park," says Eck. "If you were late with the rent, he'd understand, but he'd descend upon you if you left your trash out or didn't mow your lawn." But, says Eck, "he had his days, and how he handled the sale was so unlike everything he was."

The protestors kept modifying the barriers, and a couple of days after the main barrier was hit, Eric Daniels drew up plans of how to improve the barriers, while leaving the access road clear. Daniels, who was still hauling wastewater to Ohio, was questioning the impact of fracking, and by now knew the protestors may have been right in how they were drawing attention to the problems. He ripped off the roof of his trailer to make signs. Residents and protestors worked together to paint the signs, the most powerful

Amanda and Chevelle Fuller

one with painted handprints of the children of the village. Another of the signs listed the jobs of the residents.

Matthew West, a sculptor and digital fabricator, helped the residents create many of the signs, banners, and mobile billboards that would go into the barrier. "We worked from 6 in the morning 'til well past 2 in the morning fabricating the riggings and structural support needed to hold such large pieces of material safely in the ground," says West. He says the protestors and residents "worked so hard and quickly because it was important to us to make sure that we responded back to the resistance from the Leonards."

The signs were part of the barrier that separated the village from Aqua America; they were also information placed as billboards adjacent to, but not blocking, the main entrance into the village. The residents and protestors had become closer during the week, but "on that day is the day we [the residents and protestors] bonded, and solidified the sense of community we had all worked to grow," recalls Dr. Lee.

Amanda Fuller, Kelly Finan, Chevelle Fuller

Lauren Zygmont and Dani Little Bear

The Riverdale Mobile Home Village was becoming a battle zone. In addition to the barriers, there was now a security tent, a command/media trailer (the one that April and Eric Daniels had owned and abandoned when they left the village), a trailer with a large red cross painted onto it that served as an infirmary (once owned by Summer Gruthoff and Brian Holt), and a trailer (still owned by Kevin June) that served as a community kitchen and a place protesters could get naps and hot showers. The command trailer and one other trailer (abandoned by Fred Kinley) also served as a place protestors could sleep.

On June 7, the Susquehanna River Basin Commission, having previously approved Aqua America's request to withdraw water from the river, disregarding the voices of residents and protestors who had gone to Harrisburg for the meeting, approved the application to distribute water. The destruction of Riverdale, says Lotorto, "could only have occurred with the approval of the Commission, which didn't seem to have any consideration for the residents."

Tuesday, June 12, 2012, was overcast with intermittent drizzles. Many of the protestors wore light rain ponchos. Only a cold heavy rain could have made this summer day any uglier than it was. Most had known they would eventually be forced to end the protest; most didn't expect it to be this day.

About 10:45 a.m., Deb Eck received a call from one of the lawyers for the Riverdale residents. He told her the police would be at the village about noon to evict the protestors, and to gather all the residents and go back to their homes to avoid being arrested. "But we didn't listen," says Eck. The seven remaining families met at the Blilers' trailer for an emergency meeting.

On site to "neutralize" the protestors were six guards from Huffmaster Security, identified on its web site as a company that is the "leading provider of strike management solutions."[37]

With the confrontation escalating, Jonathan Sidney, a recent graduate of Oberlin College, did his best to reduce the tensions. For four hours, Sidney and others chatted amiably with the security team, asking questions, chatting about this and chatting about that, helping assure there would be no need for confrontation. They took the guards on a walk-through of the village.

Like the residents and protestors, the guards were working class individuals, trying to survive in an economy that was only beginning to recover; one had said he was upset about being sent to evict homeowners, having once gone through eviction himself. Others, says Matthew West, were less sympathetic "but were respectful" to protestors and residents; none wanted confrontation.

Shortly after noon, State and local police—about two dozen with handcuffs attached to their belts and an assortment of weapons—and representatives of various companies working in the Marcellus Shale showed up at Riverdale, determined to end the protest and secure the property.

Less confrontational, four persons hired by Aqua America were brought onto the grounds to install a plastic orange fence around the property. A simple job became complicated, however, because the men had begun to place the fence about 20 feet into a right-of-way. "We pointed it out to them," says Jackie Wilson, "and they had to get a surveyor's map to find the property line. The men then put metal fence posts into the ground, while others stayed close, not interfering but not helping. But Wilson had a form of protest many others didn't have. She was 64, and an activist from Occupy Harrisburg, who had camped out 10 of the 12 days of the Riverdale occupation. She didn't have to say anything to the men. "She would look at the four men with a look of contempt that suggested, 'Does your mother know what you're doing?' " says Dr. Lee.

Eck, as had been her role the past month, was all over the village, chatting with residents, protestors, the security force, and the police, doing her best to keep lines of communication open and not allow what could have been a confrontation. The protestors had no plans to become violent; the police had no reason to know that.

About 1:30 p.m., a State Police trooper asked Eck's help to end the protest. "We want to resolve this peacefully without arrests," she remembers the trooper telling her. But, she also remembers being told that the police had every intention to arrest and jail every one of the protestors. The trooper asked her to talk with the protestors and request they abandon the village.

"We had a verbal agreement with Aqua, and a lot of help and publicity about our situation," Eck says, "and I didn't want to see anyone arrested." With the police determined to handcuff and remove every protestor, Eck says she saw no way the arrests would continue to help their cause. "The money everyone, including the protestors, raised for us should now be used to help the residents, those who had already left Riverdale and the ones who remained, and not for bail money," she says.

Throughout the 12-day protest, the State Police did not confront the protestors, but showed up now and then to assure there would be no violence or destruction of property. Several residents say the State Police were polite but firm; a couple of protestors believe they were too firm, too brusque. This time, the police told the protestors they could continue their protest, but not the occupation. They had to take down the barriers and if they wished to exercise their First Amendment rights, it would have to be on a berm outside the village.

More confrontational was "Skip" Leonard. On that last day of the protest, Dr. Lee says he told her, "If you don't stop taking pictures, I am going to shove that fucking camera up your fucking ass." Dr. Lee says she responded, "Are you threatening me, Mr. Leonard?" He replied he was. "I was really upset," Leonard later said, "after 10 days, every time you turn around there was someone with a camera in your face. It gets to you." Dr. Lee says although a State Police trooper saw the incident, he walked away. She says the State Police refused to accept a complaint or to issue an incident number. She says an officer

from the Jersey Shore Police later told her that she could go to the station to file a complaint.

"We held up our banner, sang, played music, passed out rolls for people to eat, talked with each other—and prepared to be peaceably arrested," recalls Dr. Lee.

About 2 p.m., Deb Eck asked the protestors to end their resistance to avoid being arrested. "Please don't ask us to stand down," Dr. Lee asked of Eck. Dr. Lee says the protestors, about 35, "were prepared to sit down, arm-in-arm in defiance of the police" and continue the protest. But the moment Eck, representing the remaining residents, asked the protestors to "stand down" they were no longer invited guests and now would be arrested as trespassers. "I did not want to give up," says Dr. Lee, "but we were obliged to follow the wishes of the residents."

Dr. Lee remembers, "Some of us cried—perhaps out of the anxiety of the day, perhaps because this beautiful experiment in community was coming to an end, perhaps because the evacuation seemed to mean that Aqua America had won. But nothing could be further from the truth."[38] The residents and the protestors hugged each other, and the 12-day occupation ended.

"We had no leverage," says Alex Lotorto, "all it took to end our protest was a call to the State Police [by Aqua] and we were done." Goliath was finally victorious.

Sarah Ross, one of the protestors and a doctoral student in comparative literature/documentary film production at the University of Washington, recalls:

"Passing through the gate to my car, I thought about how quickly we forged a very real community made up of residents, their families, volunteers, and neighbors. We planted gardens, constructed outdoor stoves, and cleaned up debris left over from trailers that had been stripped for parts to give families some extra cash for the moving expenses. I thought about how we incorporated roofs and any building materials into the murals, so that even the physical components of the park contributed in promoting the preservation of this community. I thought about how "home" means more than a house—it is comprised of people, it is the land upon which we thrive. Many of us grew up on the Susquehanna River. And, then I thought about how our home had been violated. The Riverdale community invited us into their home, and in twelve short days, it had become ours. I thought about how quickly they tore it down. They [Aqua] threw over our barricades covered in children's handprints, and then they erected a physical dividing line between the residents and all of us."[39]

There was also another dividing line, one not formed from barriers. For years, village residents had formed a loose neighborhood; they were friends and acquaintances. They had picnics and, like residents of all neighborhoods, they sometimes had arguments or just didn't associate with other residents. But, the stress of dealing with Aqua and the forced evacuation led to an increase of rumor and innuendo, with some of the residents verbally challenging others. Everyone was frustrated and tired, their emotions bled raw by dealing with a corporate entity and issues they didn't fully understand. The division also separated those who remained from those who had taken the $2,500 and left. Those who stayed wanted to negotiate a larger moving settlement not only for themselves but also for those who had already moved. But, poor communication, combined with stress and frustration, left those who already moved feeling as if they were abandoned, first by the owner, then by Aqua America, and now by their neighbors.

"I knew this day was coming," said Kevin June, "some of us had to focus on getting out of here as soon as possible, moving on with our lives and trying not to look back."[40]

For the night of the vigil and the succeeding 12 days of the occupation, the protestors were in the village as invited guests. Each day, drivers honked in support as they drove past on Route 220; each day, the protestors drew additional attention to the problems a small community faced as they struggled to force a corporation to acknowledge that its original terms were unreasonable and needed to be revised.

Late that day, the remaining residents gathered the supplies and possessions hastily left by the protestors and handed them over the recently-constructed fence; a few, protestors and residents, openly wept. The longest around-the-clock continuous protest against fracking and for residents was now over.

At 7 a.m. of what would have been the fourteenth day, demolition crews came into the village to take down the barricades and some of the trailers. That's when Alex Lotorto figured out that Aqua America, Range Resources, or the Allan A. Myers Co., contracted to do the demolition, had not conducted an asbestos inspection required by federal law.[41] Lotorto says because he had worked with asbestos, he was aware of the problems and the regulations.

On June 21, nine days after Aqua took full possession, and after repeated calls to the Department of Environmental Protection, the DEP finally sent an inspector to the former village. "He did a cursory inspection," Dr. Lee believed, so she filed a formal complaint. On July 9, the DEP sent Dr. Lee a letter claiming it didn't find any asbestos left in the trailers or on the grounds. "There was no way asbestos wasn't present in some of

the trailers," Lotorto says. The asbestos "could have settled into the ground and was then buried," he says. Even if the DEP found asbestos, the residents were told they wouldn't be allowed to pursue a suit against Aqua America because the residents stripped the trailers and also smoked.

Destruction of a community begins in June 2012.

But, there was an even bigger truth that floated not just over Riverdale but the entire state as well. It would be a truth that would continue to establish the cozy relationship between the DEP, a regulatory agency, and the industry it was to regulate. Dr. Lee, who received the official explanation from the DEP, says Andrea Ryder, district supervisor for air quality assurance, told her, "Our job is to educate, not to penalize; we're trying to get people to do it right the next time." Thus, even if there had been open asbestos piles, with the knowledge of the new owners of the former village, there likely would not have been any fines or penalties for violating public health laws.

The second potluck picnic with protestors and former residents, held outside the village on June 17, was the last official event. By then, many of the protestors had maxed out their credit cards to buy food and supplies for themselves and the residents and former residents. But it wasn't a separation; protestors and residents stayed in touch, checking on each other.

PART 5
JULY 2012

Aqua America got what it wanted, but it was still giving residents problems. It demanded everyone who left their trailers in the village to give Aqua America clear title. It forbid any of the former protestors from coming into the village to help the residents move. Aqua America also demanded that in addition to excluding the former protestors, only family members could help, and directed Huffmaster Security to record the license plates and car descriptions of anyone who tried to help.

On July 7, the day before Deb Eck was to remove her trailer from the land that Aqua America now owned, a Huffmaster security guard told her she couldn't bring her mover onto the grounds, "that only my family would be allowed to help." This led to an angry call by the Rev. Leah Schade to Aqua America. The next day, a security guard told her that a professional mover would be allowed to assist. Eck had to call off work, and arrange not only for the move but also for others to temporarily care for her five cats and two bearded dragons, all of which she had rescued.

Denise and Scott Bliler asked for an extension to move because Scott was about to have open heart surgery, July 2, to replace an aortic valve. But, Aqua America did not allow that extension. The Blilers had to be out of the village by July 12. No exceptions. Scott Bliler came home from the hospital July 6, but was under doctors' orders not to do any work. Denise's boss had allowed her to take three weeks off, reducing some of her stress. Some of her friends, her son Robbie, and some of his friends helped. "They were awesome," says Denise, who proudly recalls that every day after work and every day Robbie was off work he and his friends would be at the trailer to do whatever they could to prepare for the move. "It was hectic and stressful," says Denise; that would be a common problem all the residents had because of Aqua America's actions. But, for Denise and Scott Bliler, there was additional stress.

On July 8, with temperatures in the 90s, and with the trailer being towed by a truck from a professional moving company, the Blilers almost managed to get their trailer out of the park safely. "All was going well," says Denise, "until we got to the gate." Because of where the chain link fence, which had replaced the orange plastic fence, was placed, and a gate that was barely wide enough to handle a 14 x 76 foot trailer, one of the biggest at Riverdale, "when the driver tried to turn onto the median to maneuver, an axle broke on the trailer." Within a couple of minutes, while on the median, the hitch broke. The trailer was towed to an automotive garage for repairs.

The last residents to leave the village were Blake and Linda Trimble, July 14, who stayed in a hotel for a month until they could find a trailer they could afford and a park that would accept them.

The residents who had stayed and negotiated with Aqua America received additional financial compensation above the $2,500 that Aqua America had originally promised. However, Aqua America forced the residents to sign a non-disclosure agreement that forbid them from talking about that settlement. The settlement, which none of the residents could talk about, required the residents not to sue Aqua America for any reason, not to be involved in any protest against the company, and not to say anything negative about the company. It also required that those who signed the settlement never speak against Aqua America for any reason at any time or else face legal action. The secret settlement is also believed to have included individual payments of about $12,000, but only for the seven families who had remained in the village after June 1. Those who left before June 1 received only $2,500. The lawyers and the seven families who stayed at Riverdale after June 1 had tried to get Aqua America to give full compensation to all families who left before June 1, but the multi-million dollar corporation wouldn't yield.

"I didn't want to sign the agreement," says Deb Eck, who wanted to wait until the report on asbestos was made public, and was upset that the non-disclosure agreement removed her rights of free speech. "That's when I was told," she says, "that if any one of the seven families didn't sign, then no one would get anything. It was all or none." Aqua representatives, says Eck, told us if we didn't sign, they would also go after everyone, including those who took the $2,500 payment and left." Eck believed it was an idle threat, just "a lot of gesturing," but she signed the agreement. "I didn't want the other six families to lose what we have worked for," she says. My pockets were heavier, but I wanted to puke."

Eck laments, "If all of us had stayed and protested, we might have been able to shut that project down or at least get them to allow us to remain." It was wishful thinking; Aqua America had made its decision, and the government planned to enforce it.

Where Riverdale once stood, construction lights have turned the night into daylight, natural vegetation is being cut down, and wildlife has been displaced. But some trailers, now little more than junk but owned by Aqua America, are still on the grounds near the Susquehanna River.

PART 6
JULY 2013

It's now been a year since the last residents left Riverdale.

A one-story 5,468 square foot green brick and concrete building that houses the pump station sits adjacent to the West Branch of the Susquehanna River. Although Aqua–PVR invested about $45.3 million into the construction of the pump station, there is no official value to the building, the miles of pipe, and the 12.16 acres of land now owned by PVR Marcellus Gas Gathering. That's because the Lycoming County assessor's office has not yet evaluated it for taxes. When it is finally evaluated, back taxes will be levied.

Beginning in February 2013, the pump station has been taking up to its allotted three million gallons of raw water from the river every day and sending it through 54 miles[42] of 12-inch diameter pipes to Range Resources and other companies that need water to frack the earth. The pipeline, Aqua America boasts, replaces about 6,000 water truck trips per day; the "boom" in Lycoming County that less than a year earlier was hailed by politicians is now reflected not only by fewer wells being drilled, but also by layoffs and terminations of drivers and auxiliary personnel.

The volume of water taken from the river has diminished because of a slowdown in drilling operations, a combination of energy companies incurring significant debt to finance their operations and a glut of natural gas because of overdrilling. Aqua–PVR pumped no water in April 2013, and less than expected the following months. Even with the slowdown, the Aqua–PVR joint venture is expected to be profitable and will show about $2.8 million in earnings in 2013, according to Nick DeBenedictus, Aqua America CEO. "If they drill, we know there will be business," he said, emphasizing, "The investment's been made, and it works."[43]

Revenue for Aqua America in 2012 was $757.8 million, a 10.3 percent increase from 2011. Net income was $196.6 million, an increase of 37.4 percent. For investors, the news was equally pleasant.[44] A 6 percent dividend increase was declared at the end of 2012; a 5-for-4 stock split was declared in the second quarter of 2013, to be applied Sept. 1. The effective dividend rate, as of the third quarter 2013, according to Aqua America, represents a 15 percent increase from the same period a year earlier.[45]

Apparently, a $150,000 fine the Department of Environmental Protection issued in May 2013 against PVR Marcellus Gas Gathering for water and ground pollution in Fall 2011 during construction of a 13-mile section of a 30-inch diameter gas gathering pipeline[46] had minimal effect upon the corporation's earnings.

The completed pumping station at what was the Riverdale Mobile Home Village.

The story of Riverdale began with the people; it ends with the people.

Kevin June, who first united the residents, has been hospitalized several times for bleeding ulcers. He is still forced to collect disability. "I can't see myself ever recovering," he says. With the settlement from Aqua America, he bought a 1988 14-by-70 mobile home with a shingle roof "in real good condition" at Harvest Moon Trailer Park, near Linden, about five miles east of where the Riverdale village once stood, and not near the river that the residents had so enjoyed. Around his trailer he has planted and tends to several flower gardens, and beams with pride when he hears others tell him it's the nicest yard in the park. The new trailer park, says June, "is nice, the neighbors are friendly, but it isn't like Riverdale."

Nine other families moved into Harvest Moon Trailer Park. Seven of the families took their trailers; all of them dipped into savings, retirement accounts, or borrowed from their families to be able to afford the move and the $100 a month higher rent at Harvest Moon. Their children would be forced to transfer school districts. Transient workers from the drilling industry live in several of the mobile homes; but as the gas drilling boom begins to subside, only about 10 or so still live in the trailer court.

Other residents eventually found spaces at other trailer parks, often renting smaller trailers; others are living in efficiency apartments, in the homes of what are now extended families; a couple of families, after years of owning their own homes, are living in senior citizen apartment buildings.

Fred Kinley, now 81, wants to move to senior citizen housing, but his pensions from Piper Aircraft and Social Security, totaling only about $1,500 a month, are too high to give him a priority on the governmental lists. And so he waits, living in a rented trailer in a non-descript trailer court, where there is no playground, no picnic area, no access to the river, and no well-kept paved roads. Traffic and wind from the dirt roads throw dust into his trailer; it's just a fact of his existence. Another fact is that "Aqua America just chopped up my trailer and threw it into a landfill," a nearly invisible tear barely noticeable in Fred Kinley's voice.

Deb Eck and her two 11-year-old daughters, who moved their trailer, live in a small no-name trailer cluster about five miles north of Riverdale. She now pays $165 more per month in lot rental.

Eric Daniels

Now unemployed is Eric Daniels, the Riverdale resident who had begun to question the effects of fracking during the protest and then became an active participant. In February 2013, Stallion Oilfield Services, the Houston-based corporation that promotes itself as "the largest provider of auxiliary rentals and services for oil and gas operations in the domestic United States,"[47] laid off 32 drivers, including Daniels, who had been with the company since November 2010. The layoffs were attributed to reduction in the need for trucks because of the Aqua America pumping station. Eric and April Daniels, and their 5- and 15-year-old daughters, live on $1,520 a month unemployment, $500 of which pays the lot rental in a trailer park that April Daniels says is "much worse" and "less safe" than Riverdale. Even if offered work in the industry, Eric Daniels won't take it—"We wanted out of the industry," says April Daniels.

However, there are other reasons why there is less work in the shale gas industry. High demands for increased production by financial institutions that had lent billions of dollars to the industry led to a glut, forcing prices well below the cost of production. The lower market prices, combined with wells that aren't producing as much as they once did, left the industry in a financial crisis. To recover, the industry has cut back on drilling, and is exporting natural gas to countries willing to pay higher prices. By selling off the reserves at higher market prices, combined with less production, the industry expects the price for domestic natural gas to rise.

Even with the slowdown of the natural gas boom, the boom that politicians and business people thought would bring lasting prosperity to the region, there are still a lot of trucks on the highways. "Every kind of truck you can imagine goes past," Deb Eck says. White pick-ups driven by managers; frack waste and brine trucks—a lot of trucks that are labeled "municipal waste." Trucks owned by the drillers; trucks owned by independent companies. One day, says Eck, her daughters "didn't feel safe getting off the school bus, so the driver stopped in the middle of the road and held back traffic until the girls got off and walked up a road to their home." But, it doesn't feel like their home. There are still unpacked boxes. "You can take a mobile home from one park, with all of its furniture, and place it elsewhere," says Eck, "but it doesn't feel like our home. We miss Riverdale. We miss the safety, the security, and the friendships."

Like most from Riverdale, Deb Eck knew little about fracking before they were evicted. And, like most, she now has become much more knowledgeable—and much more bitter.

Drifters and managers from the gas drilling industry and their vendors come into Deb Eck's store. "I try to be polite," she says, "but it's hard." The workers buy windshield washer antifreeze by the case, even in warm weather. "I asked one why so much antifreeze," says Eck, "and he said they add it to the lines to keep the drills from freezing. They also buy a lot of liquid soap for the same reason." All of that stuff, she says, somewhat sadly, "is poison. It goes into our ground." But it's their purchase of bottled water, often clearing the shelves of all bottles and cases, that brings out her strongest anger. This isn't the water they use to frack the wells, this is drinking water. She says she wants to yell at everyone who buys water by the case, "You come here and poison our water, destroy our land, and you take our clean water." She doesn't say it, but the rage builds every time she politely sells them cases of water.

Deb Eck and Kevin June, once neighbors and friends, no longer talk with each other. Some of it is the reality they no longer live in the same village; some of it is personal; much of it is because the stresses and internal politics that had torn them apart during the five months that had destroyed the park.

For five months, the struggle against eviction had brought the residents closer than they had ever been; those five months also tore them apart. There continue to be bad feelings between those who took the $2,500 and left by June 1, and those who stayed, became part of a larger protest, and eventually got larger settlements. But for most, the residents understand why some took the money and left, and why other stayed. The 32 families that were a small community have moved on, their community now destroyed.

"Once in awhile, in town I'll see one of the residents; we'll chat," says Eck. "Sometimes we'll send messages on the computer," she says.

But it's not like it ever was.

CODA

In May 2012, the Pennsylvania House of Representatives had passed an amendment (HB 1767[48]) to the Manufactured Home Community Rights Act (P.L.1176, No. 261[49]) to benefit residents of mobile home parks who are forced to move. State Rep. Robert Freeman (D-Northampton) says he had originally sponsored the bill because the Barbosa Trailer Park in Bethlehem Twp. was sold to a developer in 2006 and the residents, many of them low-income, were given only 30 days to move.[50] Rep. Freeman had introduced a bill shortly after the sale was announced, but the bill never moved onto the House floor for a vote in five years. He says because the bill was controversial, "We had been in constant negotiation with the industry and advocates since then." The current bill was introduced in June 2011, languished in a Republican-controlled committee, and may have finally been brought to the floor not only because of a successful compromise between owners and tenants associations but also because of what had been happening with Riverdale that made the public and legislators more aware of the problems. The House passed the bill, 190–7; the Senate passed it 49–0, and it was signed into law in October 2012.[51] Known as Act 156, the law requires manufactured home community owners to:

- inform residents within 60 days of any decision to close the community;
- inform the Pennsylvania Housing Finance Agency and the home municipality also within 60 days;
- give residents at least six months to leave the community when the closure notice is made
- consider any offer to purchase the community by a resident association representing at least 25 percent of the manu-

factured home spaces;

- pay relocation expenses of up to $4,000 for single and $6,000 for multi-section manufactured homes;
- pay at least $2,500 or the home's appraised value, which-ever is greater, when the homeowner is unable or unwilling to relocate the home; and
- allow tenants to terminate any leases without penalty after receiving the community's closure notice.
- that a judicial process be followed in determining when a mobile home was abandoned.

None of the families from Riverdale Mobile Home Village will be able to take advantage of the legislation.

History will record they were just collateral damage.

About the Author:

Walter M. Brasch, Ph.D., is an award-winning journalist and the author of 17 other books, most of which fuse historical and contemporary social issues. He is author of the syndicated social issues column, "Wanderings," and host of the syndicated radio show, "The Frack Report." He is featured columnist for *Liberal Opinion Week*, senior correspondent for the *American Reporter*, and senior editor for *OpEdNews*.

Among his books are *Fracking Pennsylvania: Flirting With Disaster*; and *Before the First Snow*, a critically-acclaimed novel, set between 1964 and 1991, that looks at what happens when government and energy companies form a symbiotic relationship, using "cheaper, cleaner" fuel and the lure of jobs in a depressed economy but at the expense of significant health and environmental impact.

He is professor emeritus of mass communications and journalism, and a former newspaper and magazine reporter and editor, and multi-screen multi-media writer–producer.

Dr. Brasch is an activist for social justice, dating to the 1960s. He is vice-president of the Central Susquehanna chapter of the ACLU, vice-president and co-founder of the Northeast Pennsylvania Homeless Alliance, and a member of the board of the Keystone Beacon Community for health care coordination. He was a Commonwealth Speaker for the Pennsylvania Humanities Council, and was active in emergency management.

He was president of the Pennsylvania Press Club and the Keystone State professional chapter of the Society of Professional Journalists, vice-president of the Pennsylvania Women's Press Association, and founding coordinator of Pennsylvania Journalism Educators. He is a member of the National Society of Newspaper Columnists, the Authors Guild, The Newspaper Guild (CWA/AFL-CIO), and the Society of Environmental Journalists. He is listed in *Who in America, Contemporary Authors, Who's Who in the Media*, and *Who's Who in Education*.

He was recognized in 2012 by the Pennsylvania Press Club with the Communicator of Achievement award for lifetime achievement in journalism and public service. Among recent writing awards are multiple awards from the National Society of Newspaper Columnists, Society of Professional Journalists,

National Federation of Press Women, Pennsylvania Associated Press Broadcasters Association, USA Book News, Independent Book Publishing Professionals Group, Pennsylvania Press Club, Pennsylvania Women's Press Association, International Association of Business Communicators, and PennWriters.

He was honored by San Diego State University as a Points of Excellence winner in 1997. At Bloomsburg University, he earned the Creative Arts Award, the Creative Teaching Award, and was named an Outstanding Student Advisor. He received the first annual Dean's Salute to Excellence in 2002, and a second award in 2007, and the Maroon and Gold Quill Award for nonfiction. He is the 2004 recipient of the Martin Luther King Jr. Humanitarian Service Award.

About the Photographer

Wendy Lynne Lee, Ph.D., a social activist, is professor of philosophy at Bloomsburg University of Pennsylvania where she has taught since 1983. Her areas of expertise include environmental philosophy, philosophy of language, feminist theory, anti-racism theory, philosophy of mind/brain, theory of sexual identity, phenomenology/post-modernism, and nonhuman animal cognition and welfare.

She has had published 47 peer-reviewed scholarly articles and essays, as well as two books: *On Marx and Contemporary Feminist Theory* and *Activism: Six Global Issues*. She is currently completing her third full-length manuscript, *Ecological Humanism: The Alternative to the Rhetoric of the Apocalypse*.

Her popular writings, based upon her academic specialties, appear in *Raging Chicken Press* and *Shaleshock*. She is a co-founder and member of the executive committee of the Shale Justice Coalition.

Dr. Lee is a member of the American Philosophical Association, Society for Women in Philosophy, and the ACLU. She has been honored by three ACLU chapter awards for citizen journalism, the Bloomsburg University Excellence in Teaching Award, and the Szechuan Thinkers Research Center Award from China's Yibin University.

Endnotes

[1] http://www.marketwatch.com/story/dep-celebrates-national-drinking-water-week-reminds-pennsylvanians-to-make-every-drop-count-2013-05-06
[2] http://stateimpact.npr.org/pennsylvania/tag/tom-corbett/
[3] http://www.legis.state.pa.us/CFDOCS/Legis/PN/Public/btCheck.cfm?txtType=HTM&se ssYr=2011&sessInd=0&billBody=H&billTyp=B&billNbr=1950&pn=3048
[4] http://stateimpact.npr.org/pennsylvania/2011/11/10/common-cause-report-details-campaign-contributions-from-drillers
[5] http://www.dnr.state.mn.us/lands_minerals/silicasand.html
[6] http://banmichiganfracking.org/?p=1483
[7] http://www.nytimes.com/2011/02/27/us/27gas.html?_r=3&pagewanted=all&
[8] http://www.energyfromshale.org/hydraulic-fracturing/marcellus-shale-gas
[9] http://www.eenews.net/stories/1059976102
[10] http://newsok.com/marcellus-natural-gas-production-expanded-in-2012/article/feed/479753
[11] http://www.postcarbon.org/reports/DBD-report-FINAL.pdf
[12] http://nyshalegasnow.blogspot.com/2010/11/contentious-bedrock-photos-of-marcellus.html
[13] http://www.portal.gov.on.ca/drinkingwater/stel01_049392.pdf
[14] http://www.njgeology.org/enviroed/newsletter/v2n1.pdf
[15] http://www.epa.gov/ghgreporting/documents/pdf/2010/Subpart-W_TSD.pdf
[16] http://www.envirobank.org/index.php?sid=5&rec=138
[17] http://www.endocrinedisruption.com/files/Oct2011HERA10-48forweb3-3-11.pdf
[18] http://www.forbes.com/fdc/welcome_mjx.shtml
[19] http://uk.reuters.com/article/2013/05/20/us-usa-water-idUKBRE94J0Y920130520
[20] http://online.wsj.com/article/SB10001424052748703739204576228823641659148.html# articleTabs%3Dcomments
[21] http://money.cnn.com/2012/08/10/news/economy/kansas-oil-boom-drought/index.html
[22] http://www.nytimes.com/2012/09/06/us/struggle-for-water-in-colorado-with-rise-in-fracking.html?pagewanted=all
[23] http://www.ceres.org/resources/reports/hydraulic-fracturing-water-stress-growing-competitive-pressures-for-water/view
[24] http://www.fractracker.org/2012/12/drilled-unconventional-wells-in-pa-by-county-and-year/
[25] https://www.aquaamerica.com/our-states/pennsylvania.aspx
[26] http://www.businesswire.com/news/home/20120430006113/en/CORRECTING-REPLACING-2000-Truck-Trips-Removed-PA
[27] http://aspe.hhs.gov/poverty/11poverty.shtml
[28] https://commerce.us.reuters.com/purchase/showReportDetail.do?docid=55145489
[29] http://www.pvresource.com/News/Press-Release-Details/2012/PVR-Partners-Announces-Completion-Of-Marcellus-Shale-Midstream-Pipeline-System-Acquisition-From-Chief-and-Announces-New-Bsoard/default.aspx
[30] http://www.saveriverdale.com/
[31] http://www.sungazette.com/page/content.detail/id/577215/Unfair.html
[32] http://www.sungazette.com/page/content.comment/id/575944/32-unit-village-no-more.html?nav=5019
[33] http://articles.philly.com/2012-04-18/business/31361933_1_fracking-trailer-park-anti-drilling/2
[34] http://articles.philly.com/2012-04-18/business/31361933_1_fracking-trailer-park-anti-drilling

[35] http://www.ragingchickenpress.org/2012/06/07/hands-across-riverdale-barricades-the-forward-facing-body-of-the-occupation/
[36] http://eidmarcellus.org/marcellus-shale/property-rights-where-do-we-draw-the-line/7918/
[37] http://huffmaster.com/
[38] http://www.ragingchickenpress.org/2012/06/14/2569/
[39] http://www.saveriverdale.com/2012/06/riverdale-after-eviction_13.html
[40] http://www.sungazette.com/page/content.detail/id/579556/-Amicable-resolution---reportedly-is-reached-with-last-home-residents.html
[41] http://www.gpo.gov/fdsys/pkg/USCODE-2009-title15/html/USCODE-2009-title15-chap53-subchapI-sec2605.htm
[42] https://www.aquaamerica.com/about-aqua/news/view-article.aspx?id=1570
[43] http://articles.philly.com/2013-05-05/business/39028594_1_marcellus-shale-joint-venture-aqua-america-inc
[44] *Ibid.*
[45] http://finance.yahoo.com/news/aqua-announces-9-percent-cash-113000930.html
[46] http://stateimpact.npr.org/pennsylvania/2013/06/03/pa-dep-fines-pipeline-company-for-spills-in-lycoming-county/
[47] http://www.stallionoilfield.com/index.php?id=34
[48]
http://www.legis.state.pa.us/cfdocs/billinfo/bill_history.cfm?syear=2011&sind=0&body=H&type=B&bn=1767
[49]
http://www.pmha.org/Portals/0/pdf/Act261ManufacturedHomeCommunityRightsActasamendedbyAct80.pdf
[50]
http://www.lehighvalleylive.com/bethlehem/index.ssf/2012/05/proposal_would_buy_time_for_mo.html
[51]
http://www.legis.state.pa.us/CFDOCS/Legis/RC/Public/rc_view_action2.cfm?sess_yr=2011&sess_ind=0&rc_body=H&rc_nbr=1397

CPSIA information can be obtained at www.ICGtesting.com
Printed in the USA
BVOW10s0201230913

331804BV00006B/9/P